KICKING ASS
AND
TAKING NAMES

Poetry through the eyes of a tough guy

Nik C. Colyer

Singing Reed books may be purchased for educational, business, or sales promotional use. For information please write: Special Markets, Singing Reed Press   228 Commercial St. #173   Nevada City, CA 95959.

Publisher's Cataloging-in-Publication
(Prepared by The Donohue Group, Inc.)

Colyer, Nik C.
    Kicking Ass and Taking Names : Poetry through the eyes of a tough guy: selections from thirty years of writing / Nik C. Colyer- 1ˢᵗ ed.
    p. cm.
    LCCN 2003115971
    ISBN   0-9708163-6-7

1. Poetry--Collections. 2. American Poetry--20ᵗʰ century--Collections.
    I. Author. II. Title: Kicking Ass & Taking Names.

PS3553.04784 K53 2004
813'.54-dc21

Thanks to my editor, Bobbie Christmas.

Printed in the United States of America.
10 9 8 7 6 5 4 3 2 1

To all of the tough guys
who have found their hearts

CONTENTS

Author's Note

The following pages come from a collection of thirty years of random thoughts and expressions usually scribbled down on paper napkins, backs of shopping lists, margins of phone bills, and scraps of paper bags. Mostly, poetry comes to me in violent outbursts of emotion that must be written down the very instant it arrives, or be lost forever.

Poetry is a fast-moving river, and I have the opportunity to dip a cupful once in a while. Without seizing the moment to dip the cup, the river moves on, and the feeling disappears.

Sometimes only a single line is retrieved and the rest of the poem must be painfully squeezed from that moment. The best poems, and you will recognize them immediately in this collection, were ones that came to me as complete expressions, when I slid to a stop on the side of the freeway or raced into the house to find paper and pen to write them down.

The job for me as a poet is to be prepared at all times for those few moments a month when lightning strikes, the river floods it banks, and the words flow in a seemingly endless list of lines, straight from the heart, separate from thought. The great poems come to me in bunches, five or six at a time, then months might go by before another good moment strikes. I may write every day, but most become fodder for the shredder.

Perhaps the job for you as the reader is to search out poems that strike deep into your heart, cherish their resonance and seek new discoveries often. A good poem might even give voice to the poet that lives inside you.

Nik

KICKING ASS and TAKING NAMES

KICKING ASS AND TAKING NAMES

I'm kicking ass and taking names
in a world that wants me to be silent.

I roll the dice while naked in the rain,
moving fast and acting insane,
feeling the bite of unstructured pain
left behind too many years ago to remember.

I'll dump the crap
and hope it's not too late
for a different kind of date
with a destiny so carefully planned,
now thrown to the wind,
for the rest of me.

10-03

BLINDSIDED AGAIN

Don't blindside me with your issues
amid our playful moments
and think I'll not notice what you've done.

Don't dismember our situation
unless you know I am ready
to face the abyss
of your every concern.

Don't casually project
inadequate feelings,
hoping I'll step into
that dangerous arena
with you.

Never again.

10-03

GIVE ME ROOM

I need room to prepare for your issues.
I want time to get up my guard.
Attack with disappointments,
I'll withdraw at the blink of an eye.

I get confused when I'm not ready,
not so much about your subject,
but about your reason why.

You must give me warning
and wait as I prepare
for the cuts and slices of your concern.

10-03

CONFUSION

Don't take what I say personally.
Don't hear my every word.
I'm speaking through a veil
without the safety net of male logic.

Instead, come float with me
into the depths of the sea
of confusion.

7-03

FLIRT

Fifty-five, and still I want to be
attractive to younger women;
you know, the pretty ones.
The desire is there as it was in youth,
but lately my body seldom follows my most
arrant command.
Yet I am still capable of flirting,
as I proved today
with my dark-eyed saleswoman.

7-03

NOT ME

Someone murdered the leaf-blower man.
I swear it wasn't me.
My neighbor, Sara, found him face down
in a lot next to the A & P.
No one understood the reason why;
he was such a nice sort of guy.
Someone murdered the leaf-blower man
early this morning under a budding tree.
His blower motor idling,
it had been, since three.
Someone murdered the leaf-blower man.
I swear it wasn't me.

3-03

THERAPEUTIC "I"

Yes, there is a place to be nice
and use the "I" message,
but, and it's a very big but,
maybe the size of Manhattan,
there is a time to screw the "I."

What happens when the rage rhino
stands pawing the sand,
singular horn poised,
ready for a charge?

I'm looking for a target,
other than you,
to place my killer ape's
repressed reptilian response.

1-03

BE NICE

I want somewhere to express my anger.
I have no container to hold my rage.
I need a location to unravel.
I must leap out of my cage.

I'll find a place to unleash emotion,
discover the spot in my soul,
fight to be free in a repressed culture
in a world that wants me under control.

1-03

WORK FOR FOOD

I'd work for food or a five-dollar job,
be happy in a rusted Chevy with no engine.
Give me a room in the Del Oro Hotel;
so what if it's for older people?
I like old people; I'll be one someday.
I'd take a dog-eared Conan novel,
over Giddian, anyway.
A black and white with no reception,
a stack of quarters to do my wash,
a bag of groceries from the Quick Stop,
a pack of Camels, don't call a cop,
and I'll be happy any day.

11-02

THE LIVING WOUND

Whether through serrated remarks
or the back of his hand,
we all live with wounds from the father.

If we found ourselves controlled
or abandoned to live on our own,
his ghost sits with his sons and daughters.

Was it simply that we loved the same woman,
our mother, his wife and ever-fading lover,
tearing us apart when we became men?

Did he survive or devour his competition,
or was it we that turned away,
rejecting the old,
tamping and trampling him
in our haste to be the future?

It's taken too many years,
but our father is forgiven
for reacting with such vengeance,
taking so personally
the inevitable strikes and blows of the son.

10-02

DEATH OF A SON

Until he was twelve,
we were the best of friends,
before his passage into manhood.
He and I stood together,
two pillars through time,
until I pressed him not to be himself,
but be like me.

I forgot he would stop leaning on his father,
reaching for my hand,
looking for acceptance.

In my busy life, I let his hand go,
forced my world upon him,
not knowing he would eventually
carve out purpose from the ashes
of the only life I've ever known.
I cut him, ridiculed him,
left him on his own.
I ignored and teased him,
then withdrew my love.
I pummeled him with limited perception,
forgetting he would continue without me,
unaware that his world grew beyond me
into a future I could not hope to comprehend.

10-02

AFRAID FOR MY SECOND NOVEL

I'm afraid that my heart and soul have poured out on these pages, and you're going to get to the hard part, put it down, then abandon it and me forever.

I'm afraid that the who I've conjured up during these winter months, sitting in front of this keyboard each morning before dawn before the birds awake, before my wife has stirred, is too much for our sheltered natures to handle.

I'm afraid that my critics are right, and I've missed the mark, missed my calling, and who am I to think that I'm a writer, after all?

What if I've gathered, page after page, of a story I did not fully understand until it was written, and you don't want to read it? What if my understanding is nothing but simply wanderings of a worn-out mind in an aging body?

I'm afraid to show you this, unchanged,
because of suggestions from those who want it
watered down in the name of marketability.

I'm afraid it's so raw that we will part
company, you, my reader, and me, those ever-
more-fleeting moments of inspiration.

Yes, there is a piece of me in this, as you will
find there is also a piece of you. It is
something that we, you and I, do not want to
look at, but it is a part of us after all, and don't
we have to live with and try to heal what
haunts us and drags us away from the things
we love?

10-02

MAMMOTH

Surrounded by a sheet
of trampled and slushy snow,
only a miniscule mound
of ignored perfection is left
of a storm two hours ago.

The rush of traffic
and careful steps of humanity
slide and slip across patterned ice,
leaving tracks of four-wheel drives
and cleated boots.

A man slips and lands hard on his back.
I hear the crunch of bones.
Almost no one slows to offer a hand on this,
of all days, hours before Christmas.

I push my finger into the mound of fluff,
deface the last remaining sign of
nature's attempt to heal the wounds
inflicted by humanity, the mall, a parking lot,
and too many frayed nerves.

12-01

POCKET CHANGE

She sits at the counter checking her assets,
like a boxer counting his falls.
She flinches with every punch and jab,
wishing it was like the old days,
spending money like water in the mall.
She's down to pocket change.
She no longer counts what's left in days.
With a wince she checks her silver once again,
change from yesterday's pack of Luckys
and a small taste of gin.
She's down to her last dollar,
a cup of coffee and a roll.
She wonders just how she'll make it through,
how she'll ever make it at all.
She considers selling her body
to get through another day,
but there ain't much left to sell,
too many hungry nights in her own little way.
She nurses her java;
it's been cold too long,
no more hope, no more refills,
making it last,
to stay out of the downpour
in another filthy restaurant
in an LA rain.

1-01

A SURPRISE MOON

For the first time, in a predawn hour,
a full moon peeks through our dense forest
with only enough glow to spotlight my desk
in a ghostly brilliance.
I pick up a pen, seldom used these days,
a simple tool for the primitive moment.
Moonlight has centered on my paper,
from the one small piece of sky.
It hangs there for a fleeting moment,
allowing me to scribble these words,
to feel like a poet again,
after a long, dry spell.
The glow is so vague, I can't read the words,
only a formless knowledge
that the pen is still writing
chicken-scratch across a blank page.
Quickly, I write before the ghost light
disappears behind another branch.
Once the elusive sliver of radiance moves on,
I'm back in the blackness of my silent forest,
back to listening to deer crunch
through frostbitten autumn leaves.
Good-bye hoarfrost light, however uncertain,
and to you, poem,
who visits the poet so seldom these days.

11-99

ELK

The ever-constant hiss of surf against sand,
crashing waves whisper long-forgotten secrets.

The effortless flight of hawks and sea birds
floating on a salt breeze.

The sun extinguishes itself into three
thousand miles of Jade Pacific, a horizon so
flat I can almost see the curve of the earth.

We draw a tub and make love
without the usual rush,
taking time for one another and finding
misplaced, but familiar spots
in each other's hearts.

An ink darkness descends
as we open windows wide,
snuggling deep under covers,
listening to surf crash against rocks
while slumbering in each other's arms.

5-99

BARKING

I have thoughts of murder
at three a.m.,
with the endless sound of
an idiot dog barking.
I'm thinking of how to do it in the darkest
hour without my neighbor knowing it was me.
I've tried to tell him;
I've tried to explain,
but he insists his dogs never bark.

4-99

STAGES

Being born is the first pain in life.
We don't realize the freedom of childhood,
until puberty overpowers adolescence.
Adulthood too soon gives way to the parent,
in the blink of an eye a grandparent.
The golden years are times of slowing,
and if our life was honorable or interesting,
if it had meaning and content,
if how we lived was worth speaking about,
the stories will continue
down through the generations.

2-99

MENOPAUSE, FIRST STAGE

I am not your enemy;
I'm your best friend.
Don't you remember?
I am not all men,
nor am I HIM,
I'm only a man.
If you want to get angry,
I say get angry. . .get angry. . .go crazy,
but don't point at me
with your lifetime of abuse.
I'm not your enemy;
I'm your best friend.
Don't you remember?
I don't need to look down the barrel
of your wrath any longer.
I don't want to fear another bullet
of your rage coming my way,
because I'm not the enemy;
I'm your best friend,
remember?

1-99

SHADOWS

At twenty-one the sun rose in my life.
At fifty-one there are many shadows.

9-98

ARTIST'S EYE

The sculptor can see only
each hammer blow that went askew
in a work that the world would call perfect.

The painter can spot the one brushstroke
out of place on an entire canvas.

The musician berates himself
for a single sour note
in an otherwise flawless performance.

The poet?
Well, the poet is never satisfied.

3-98

GANGBANGER

We search for honor
in a world devoid of such things.
We seek a guiding code for which to live,
with television as our only muse.
We look for meaning,
without help from an elder.
We don't even know an elder
who deserves our respect.
So we find a teenage version of masculinity,
a code created by others like ourselves,
a code created without the wisdom
years of living can bring.

3-98

A WOMAN IN HER POWER

My heart flies into a jealous rage,
for the first time in my life.
The first time I've cared enough,
the first heartache,
and all without a cause.

With determination, I try
to mend my broken soul,
to tell myself you are still with me,
and there's no reason to cry.

Yet my body freezes when I see you,
I mean really see you
standing alone in your power.
My logic tells me
there is no basis for my fear;
still, from across the room, I start to die.

My deepest terror is that you are leaving,
and yet I know you are not gone,
though my heart is still bleeding,
still reaching and clutching,
for I am drowning.
I reach for a straw,
the lifeline of your love.

11-97

TURNS

All hope is shattered
the moment she turns aside.
All love is lost
when she stops looking in my eyes.
The memory of her still lingers.

11-97

SHE SAYS

I will continue to love you,
but only if I stay in my power, she says.
I will stick around with integrity
and be with you only if I remain strong,
she says.

I will only love you
from my womanly passion,
not my needy little girl, she says.
I am no longer looking
for someone to save me, she says.

11-97

THE EVER-PERFORMING MALE

My trial and sentencing as a man
continues in my ability to pretend
that I know how to have sex with a woman
without performing.

When I let go of my
tried and true little tricks,
my pathetic, well-versed bells and whistles,
when I release my need
to please her at any cost,
I find my gangly, nervous teenager
next to someone I've never known,
myself.

When I cease my incessant search for the goal,
I find my body and heart are numb.

11-97

ACCEPTED

Our tears flow like hot water,
our love waxes and wanes like the moon
with each stroke of my maleness,
which you accept then release
and open like a flower.

We find our moment after an hour,
enveloping our merging souls
in this caldron of loving each other.
For the first time in my life,
for the very first time,
I've truly been received by a woman.

11-97

TOO OLD TO DREAM

I'm finding hidden tracks of love wounds
strung out behind me in long processions
of broken and disabling affairs.

Filling the holes left behind from you,
elongated chasms stretched so far
they look like mere creases
in the fabric of time.

I keep my guard up high, so high, too high,
a shield from the razor, a dagger,
or darning needle; it doesn't matter.
A weapon might come out of nothingness
or out of my past
with the speed of a bullet,
to pierce my heart.

9-97

THE HAG

Why would you assume
men don't know the hag?
What makes you think
she doesn't visit us
every day of our lives?

Why would you present the question,
when the hag is present on every street,
in the check-out at the grocery,
our teachers,
our lovers,
our mothers.

She'll smack us with the back of her hand
or strike with doubled fist;
there's nothing we can do.

The worst of all nightmares,
she'll open up a gash
straight to our heart
with her razor words.

9-97

MEMORIES

We had memories of good times and tired old jokes, the last vestiges of a coherent crowd trying desperately to have a conversation.

9-97

LAKES IN MINNESOTA

Ten thousand lakes in Minnesota,
ten thousand days of snow and rain,
ten thousand lush, green meadows,
forgotten memories of the great plains
ten thousand years ago.

Ten thousand lakes in Minnesota,
ten thousand siloed farms,
ten thousand ears of corn per acre,
yet not enough to feed the land.

Ten thousand lakes in Minnesota,
ten thousand houses around each one,
ten thousand pounds of pesticides
on ten thousand manicured lawns.

8-97

FRIENDS

Some friends come out of the woodwork
when we are desperate.
Some hide out until the storm is over.
Some friends stick close,
sit tight, and wait with us.
The rest, well, the rest,
too quickly become associates.

8-97

DEATH WATCH IN SEATTLE

She's slipping away,
inch by incremental inch,
as she also lived her life.
We stand death watch in the hospital,
with lines and tubes to support a body
that gave up a month ago.

I see death in her eyes,
but she doesn't even know it.

She's dying in Seattle
in a sterile hospital bed,
with stale air and noisy machinery
to keep her company.
If there is a hell,
it's to die in this room.

6-97

DANGER, WILL ROBINSON

She's in one of those dangerous buying
moods.
She'll raid Nordstrom's and Macy's
before the day is out.

4-97

KLUTZ

I try to nail together two boards,
and there are too many moving parts.
I try to put together two words,
and the sentence is too long.

4-97

GHOST OF THE FATHER

Every time I open my mouth,
the ghost of my father comes out.
Every time I think a thought,
he shapes my every moment.
Every time I make a move,
I see him moving next to me,
directing my every turn.
Every time I think I'm acting on my own,
he's standing there, acting for me.
Every time I open my mouth,
the voice of my father slips out.
Every time I open my mouth,
my father jumps out.
Every time,
my mouth,
he's out.

4-97

FORGOTTEN GAS

It sits alone and forlorn
next to an abandoned highway that carried
a full load of traffic twenty years ago.
It's lost and forgotten,
now that the freeway passes
high on the hill overhead.
Unkempt and unpainted,
the pumps haven't seen gasoline in a
generation.
Rusted shells of automobiles,
abandoned then slowly stripped,
sit behind the building,
barely hiding the fact
that time has moved on.

3-97

WOODSTOVE

We have a new woodstove in our house,
the kind with a big glass door.
It takes the place of TV here at home,
as we sit for hours watching the fire,
more interesting than TV
could ever hope to be.
I feel much closer to my ancestors
who also sat over a flickering blaze,
talking and chanting in the frigid night,
only the crackling flame to keep them warm.

1-97

TEARS

Down under anger into my grief, I go
deep under the layers to my tears,
and finally to a peaceful place in my soul.

These are the same tears that frightened me,
the same tears I now joyously shed,
acknowledging, after so long,
that I can feel my heart again,
closed so many years.

12-96

MY FATHER AND HIS LIFE

Finally, after forty-eight years,
after I gave up on any hope that he
would ever reveal his life to me, suddenly,
for no apparent reason,
my father, who speaks in single syllables,
spends three hours telling me of his life.
He talks of the days of his past,
his women, the war,
success and failures, his jobs.
When it is over,
he never says another word.

11-96

SHADOWS

My shadow cast long and lean
in the afternoon of my life.
It's more easily seen,
now that I'm standing in full light.
Even the darkest corners
that lie hidden in my soul
seem less than the darkness of a closed heart.

10-96

A LIFE NOT KNOWN

My grief is felt,
not for what I know,
but what I do not.
I'm sad for the loss
of what I do not understand.
I feel a pain in my heart from a life,
maybe not without knowing,
but more of not being known.

10-96

UNWILLING

I touch the underbelly of my soul.
I'm touching my thoughts,
my truth, my right.
I'll touch something
I no longer can control,
a demon monster who's
been hidden forty-eight years.
I'm no longer able to contain
something thick and hard,
an unwilling part of my pain.

10-96

I WANT TO

I want to stay with you,
but only when I want to.
I want to see the you in you,
but only when I want to.
I can't help but love you,
but only when I want to.
I like it when I touch you,
but only when I want to.
You may say I'm selfish, too,
but only when you want to.

10-96

THE FACE OF MY FEAR

I hadn't shed a single tear in a last half year.
I didn't want to feel that something
or someone who frightened me.

For days my tears have rolled,
flooding my sorrow,
stuck deep in my heart,
yet I still don't know the face of my fear.

I want to put a woman's face on my fear,
a face I try to recognize,
an illusive face I might love.

Once I saw this ghostly face in the dark,
looking back at me from a mirror.

10-96

THE LAST ECLIPSE OF THE MILLENNIUM

We lay entwined in one another's arms
as the last eclipse of the millennium
casts a silver glow between a thick forest,
shines through the window,
and spreads across our bed.

A ghostly glow mirrors off our bodies
as we move and shift to get comfortable
during a warm, late autumn night.

I awake often to witness the moon
traverse an inky sky
with shadows of an alpine spruce
to obscure an already muted iridescence.

I remember a secret touch in the night
during one moonlit awakening,
kissing, murmuring,
primitive sounds of mating,
under the soft glow
of a harvest moon
during the last eclipse of the millennium.

9-96

HOPES OF A WORKING MAN

I worked eighty-nine hours last week
loading lumber at the mill,
hanging with the boys after work.

I work my butt off every day,
because I got two kids and a wife,
you see, and I'm proud to say
I'm a better man for it.

For eight years, Sheila and I
tried to make it work.
When she left, she said
I was never was around.
I was around!

I see my girls once a month
for two hours or so.
They live in Bishop with their mom.
I wish she lived closer,
so I could see my girls.

8-96

A STORY TOLD MORE THAN ONCE

I met a guy that knows a guy
who knows Arnold. You know,
Schwarzenegger, in the movies.
I know a guy who knows a guy
who knows Arnold.
I know a guy who knows Arnold.
I once met Arnold.
I know Arnold.
We're the best of pals.

8-96

WHERE IS YOUR WARRIOR?

You give lip service to warrior training,
standing with pride with shaman abilities,
looking down your nose at the rest of
humanity.

You speak of your leadership
in powerful circles, and that may be so,
but I look in your scared rabbit eyes
and see a frightened little boy.
Where is your warrior?

7-96

A YOUNG MAN AND THE YUBA

A woman lies naked in the summer sun,
stretched long on a granite boulder.
She stands and takes a look around,
then dives into an emerald river.

She's unaware of a young man's heart.
He stands alone in the shadow,
admiring her from afar,
wanting her to really see him.

His eyes caress her nakedness;
his chest breathes her scent.
At night he has sex dreams of her willingness,
certain she'll never know
of his longing heart.

6-96

ANSWERING MACHINE

She's having relationships
with men's answering machines,
calling them only when she's sure
they're not at home.
She doesn't answer when they call,
but listens to the message,
placing her wishes and dreams
on what they say to her machine.

6-96

FOILED BY MAN

The best laid plans of women for their men
are plots devised as a little girl.
She lay in wait after years of longing
for the he that will be like her,
for a yielding man
like the teddy bear she once loved.
Her best laid plans are foiled by a man.

5-96

MY WITCH

I'll take my witch back now, thank you;
you've carried it much too long.
I'll steal my zeal to be nice to you
and wonder what went wrong.
I'll rob you of the bitch that is mine
given to you,
I don't know why,
I don't know how,
I don't know when,
but I take my witch back now.
Thank you.

5-96

THE HERO

I've carried the flag of battle
for a world who looked to me
to cry outraged against injustice.
I was the first to call foul,
when authority was unfair,
to fight oppression when
others rolled over in submission.

I was also the first to spot the inept,
of which there were many.

I gladly held the hero's stance,
to face the cold rejection of authority,
but I'm ready to pass the baton,
for the hero no longer serves me.

4-96

GOOD-BYE MR. NICE GUY

A thunderous rage
rolls up from deep inside my gut,
unbridled from a long constricted core.
A hailstorm of resentment
without restitution
takes possession of me.

I feel like busting all the glass
and kicking some ass,
dismembering anything
unable to move away fast.
But it won't be enough
to relieve a lifetime
of concealed rage.

My stored feelings of the Neanderthal,
who strikes out to ease a ball of fury,
held too long as a constrained fire in my belly.

For thirty or forty years it has been hidden
under the guise of what my women
could only cherish as Mr. Nice Guy.

4-96

MISTER MUSIC

His sound was alive and full of promise,
a short dozen years ago.
With guitar in hand,
his voice was so fresh and clear,
he brought tears to my eyes.
His chiseled features
left women groveling,
begging for another song, another moment,
in another time, not so long ago.
Tonight he drones out worn, ragged tunes.
His soulful beat once in abundance,
lifeless and broken now,
playing only for his pay,
when once he played just to play.
He's an old man before fifty and I wonder
what, besides time, turned him.
Was it too many bars,
playing for nickels and dimes,
or the defeat from
an expected life under the lights?
Drugs, it was whispered,
left a face flat and dead,
embossed in a gray and lifeless world,
when only a few years ago,
he played so light and strong.

12-95

THE FATHER WOUND

Wounded early by the father,
I've been hobbled almost fifty years.
I was stabbed deeply by his distance,
while living in his domain,
under his thumb,
with his hidden rage.

I was hurt deeply by the father,
wiped out sometimes by a single word,
with only a mother to protect me,
enraged that she was there,
and at myself when I ran to her.

I'm injured by the father,
by his inability to be around,
not able to see that I needed
his strength, his wisdom.

I'm reminded of the father,
left outside the men's world,
never included in a masculine realm,
always secluded,
a child away from the men.

10-95

TELEGRAPH AVENUE

Our sons and daughters
come to visit the sidewalks and steps
of the heart of the revolution,
some thirty-odd years ago.

They step lightly over the same concrete,
through once-burning buildings,
on fire with the change of the times.

The winds of change are breathless, now,
and feeling hopeless with age and neglect.
Political science sections,
once in front windows of every bookstore,
lay untouched in dusty, dark, back corners.

They sell T-shirts and sweatshirts, now,
with tired, recycled logos; peace and love,
all but distant memories of a
glorious time of upheaval.

The ghost of a turbulent past,
too much left undone,
too many heroes dead too many years ago
for the young to care to remember.

12-94

RENEGADE

A renegade wind rolls fast and hard
across a silent desert floor.
A tidal wave of air,
bent on destruction,
intent on mayhem,
cuts a wide path
through the cactus and sage,
tears loose and tosses into the air
a wall of rubble rolling toward me.
From a distant rise,
like a gigantic feather pillow,
not noticeably moving at all,
it approaches faster than I realize.
I turn away to look for shelter,
then hear a whine that
travels fast over open terrain.
I close my eyes,
throw myself to the ground,
as dust and debris howl over me.
The storm lasts a minute, then
leaves the desert floor silent again.

8-93

LOVE LOST

I'm here, my heart in my throat,
my face twisted into a comical grin.

I'm still here, waiting again
for you to throw me a splinter
of a small bone of your love.

You turn after touching my shoulder,
then disappear into the crisp spring night.

I walk the other way, angry at myself
for being so weak and sucked in again
to the possibility of your love.

4-93

PLASTIC SMILE

I slip through the cracks of love,
sit on the backside of romance,
go through the motions alone,
walk around in a daze,
a plastic smile pasted to face the world.

4-93

VACANCY

There's a big hole in my heart
where tears flow through,
a long vacant lot where you once stood.
I can't get a hold of my life,
now that you are gone;
can't seem to find a reason why.

4-93

DELUSIONS

All of a sudden,
far off in the distance,
like a freight train racing through my heart,
I came to understand;
you wanted to be in love with me
much more than you were.

4-93

REGULAR SORT OF GUY

I don't want to be your hero;
I'd have too far to fall.
Please don't place me so high.
I'm only a regular sort of guy.

I will no longer be your superman,
though you look for that in every man.
The dad you never had does not exist,
so give me a kiss good-bye;
if you insist on placing me that high.

1-93

TAKING CUES FROM WOMEN

As a young man I tried to understand
since my hormones began.
I've followed, puppy-dog-faced,
attempting to reason
what drives me.

All of my trying, just to get laid;
All of this concentration for sex?
It now seems so overrated.

10-92

BROADWAY

It's been fifty, maybe a hundred years,
since the Broadways of America
have been avenues of style.

The rotting buildings, once places to be,
lay in ruin, barely held together
with broken promises.

Under flaking paint and boarded windows,
the grand style parades,
a past of grace and wonder,
a time of expensive cars and stylish women.

Now we drive the streets only if we must,
our doors securely locked.
Now homeless sleep humiliated and ignored
in littered doorways and filthy back alleys.

The stench of urine and the sadness
of a dismal present fill the air,
with no promise of a future.

Broken humans wander the sidewalks
beg for spare change to get through
another day or another bottle.

10-92

LOST VALUES

What's happened to our values?
Disappeared in the ghostly screens of TV.
Where do we put our misplaced honor?
We've asked the Rambos of the world
to carry it for us, and they are glad to.
What of those elusive morals
we thought we once had?
Given to the evangelist,
who steals money for his crusade.

Left with the anger and frustration
of our self-imposed oppression,
we seek pointless icons to fill the holes
in our empty and unnatural modern lives.

7-92

PAM

You make me dream beyond my means.
I find myself discontent
with the best life I've ever known.
You make me want
much more than I've ever seen,
unable to remember
what it was
I'd decided to do
before I met you.

12-91

WILDNESS

Lizards, snakes, and birds
snatched from the floor of the jungle,
imported for the spoiled children
of North American urban dwellers.

Captured and stolen for profit,
sold to humans unwilling or unable
to honor the uninhibited lives
of the creatures of the jungle.

Do people hope that owning the wild thing
will awaken their own naturalness
long ago surrendered
to the comforts of the hearth
and more recently relinquished
to an industrial age?

Finally and painfully,
through changing childhood fantasies
from too many months of neglect,
the wild creature dies and is
disposed of, without thought,
like old chicken bones.

12-91

COUNTING

I can count on one hand
the times in my life
I've been sexually fulfilled.
I'm not speaking about fleeting satisfaction,
for those have been countless.
I'm talking about having a woman interested
long enough that sex isn't in deficit,
long enough that I can relax into a
relationship, to feel the comfort of a woman
who wants me.

9-91

SEX; A WOMAN'S LAST STRONGHOLD

When all of her power has slipped away,
she feels weak and helpless.
A woman still has her sex over men
to get their attention,
or the absence of sex over her man
to get his attention,
or get even.

9-91

ANGER

You have a right to your anger,
but no right to dump it on me.
I applaud your need to express it,
just don't expect that I'll be
around so you can abuse me.

A shield of indifference is my only protection
from your stiletto words stabbing my heart.

As you can tell, I'm still slow to the test.
I look with surprise and wonder,
as trickles of blood dribble from my chest.

9-91

GETTING NUMB AGAIN

My memory of why
it was so important
to make these changes
has slipped through
calloused fingers
as time slides away.

This path I have chosen
shows itself only in my future.

By the time the why of my choice
comes full term, the veils of a failed memory
leave me numb again,
vulnerable to the next situation.

8-91

ONLY ONE DINNER WITH JEAN

A hidden blowtorch of anger
permeates the pores of your skin.
Like rolling, dripping beads of sweat,
concealed fury comes from within.
I sit across the table in polite conversation
watching your rage puddle on the carpet,
then spread its tentacles toward me.

I stand, step back, notice it
again come toward me
in waves that roll across the floor.
I step back once more,
turn, and find myself running,
your bitterness nipping at my back,
attempting to chase me down
and stab me one hundred times
for something someone else did
to so deeply wound your spirit.

6-91

YOUR HAPPINESS

There is nothing I can do to make you happy;
you would only resent me for it later if I tried.
I know you want me to fill your emptiness,
but it is only you who can do it for yourself.

4-91

DEFIANCE

You stand there with a defiant glare;
Me, I sit here beaten
from months, maybe years
of the subtle oppression of your love.

I have known that you love me
as much as you can,
but so many strings come with that love
now knotted together into
one large, ragged rope,
strangling me.

I've taken a razor,
hacking and slashing
at each individual string,
attempting to unravel your subtle threads.

Unfortunately, mounds of rope
lay on the floor between us,
trampled and sliced into pieces.

4-91

LOST DREAMS OF AN OLDER MAN

She steps lightly in this world
but leaves a wide swath
of destruction in her wake.
She holds me and loves me for a moment
then runs, looking for a younger man.
My dream of her shatters,
but don't we all dream
of the one who gets away,
the phantom lost love
with only false memories
to keep us alive.

4-91

LAST CHANCE AT
A STOP CALLED YOUTH

A last look at my vanishing youth,
one last chance to live that way again.
One final, wild fling,
as she stepped into my world.

The freshness of her innocence
infecting me,
reminding me of a time
when my body moved much faster,
joints not stiff from the cold.

I stopped there for a month,
long enough to remind me
of the gulf of time between us
on the last chance at a stop called youth.

4-91

I'M A MAN

I want to do everything to make you happy,
I just don't know what to do.
I want to show my love to you through action.
I'm a man; it's what I do.
I seem to miss the mark,
fail in your eyes.
I don't know if it's mistakes I've made,
or your standards are too high.

12-90

MS. RUSTY

It was the best sex I ever had,
and we hardly touched.
It was one special moment in time.
How did I know it would never come again?

You caressed me with long, crimson hair,
whispered in my ear,
then left me tingling with anticipation.

We had only a moment or two,
then I was gone,
thinking I could return anytime.

Tonight I came back,
some six months later,
and, of course, you were gone,
another fantasy to haunt me
the rest of my life.

3-89

CLOSE

It's so easy to get close,
but so hard to back away.
It's so easy to let love tangle my heart,
but so hard when it's been cut to shreds.

11-87

BACK FROM VEGAS

I'm driving north out of Vegas,
radio blasting to stay awake,
in an uphill pull
two hundred miles to Tonopah.
The glitter of the city that never sleeps
falls away behind me
into the darkness of the desert.
The road is so straight,
I see oncoming headlights
for thirty miles.
No surprises.
No surprises.
Not even interesting road kill.

9-87

DESERT

Desert flowers bloom overnight.
The desert floor is alive again.
The freshness of the rain and morning dew
makes life seem soft and gentle,
these few desert moments
before the burn of summer.

3-87

MONEY

This is the first time in my life
that money flows like a river.
I still don't understand how
to handle or spend it,
when to hold it, and
when to let it go.

8-86

MS. B

Stumbled across a photo the other day,
you and me sitting together.
I couldn't help but remember
the short time we spent with each other.

Stumbled across a memory the other day
it left me to wonder
how we loved so hard and fast,
then lost each other.

Stumbled across some tears the other day,
old broken mementos I thought I'd forgotten.
I quickly put them away.

10-84

LIVING IN TERROR OF MY CAR

I open the door,
hope the handle works,
insert the key carefully,
so the ignition doesn't jam.
At the moment of contact,
I wish I could be sure.
In the summer the seats scald.
During winter months,
I wade my way
to the pedals,
being careful not to crush
mushrooms colonizing
what's left of the carpet.

2-83

ARTIST'S RESUME

I work in:
clay, steel, iron,
walnut, wax, wood, and fire,
glue, gloves, grit, grime,
copper, bronze, gold, and mire,
silver, stainless, marble, glass,
garnets, ruby, diamonds, some cash,
onyx, abalone, alabaster, and then I mix,
words of wit and musical writ.

12-81

THE FARMYARD JUNKPILE

History in the raw,
garbage and junk cars,
bolts and bicycle wheels,
tell the story too well,
of unwanted toys,
and broken tools.
The last generation's wares
left as this year's junk,
to be carted off as tomorrow's antiques.

8-81

OLDER

The Doris Days are getting older;
rinses, dyes, paints, and powder
don't help make her younger
than her gray-haired friends anymore.

She's starting to sag at the corners,
once so sweet a smile
now tight with contempt,
for the young twits
who hang out like she used to.

She stumbles in her walk,
with a slur to her talk
from the pills the doctor gave,
to take away the pain of getting old.

7-81

DARK STORIES

Dark stories
around the fire
deepen the shadows
of the outside edge.

Old men talk,
while stories dance
in the flicker of the blaze.

1-81

LIFE

Life was wild and crazy
when I was young and strong,
but it didn't last long;
now it's just hazy.

It was easy to love and leave
when I was young and strong,
just walk away and not look around.

7-80

VOYEUR

Here I am watching,
each one looking
at each one watching
another.

Our eyes never meet,
while we all watch,
without being seen.

1-80

WORKING MAN

Forty years
going to work,
watching TV,
drinking beer,
once in a while
out on the town.

What do you have left?
A worn-out body,
and a dull mind.

Too much drink,
too much work,
not enough time to think,
but who takes the time?
Who has the time, anymore?
Only us unemployed poets.

1-80

JENNY

We cried our tears
and tried to tear
apart before
it got too strong,
but we stayed too long,
too long, too long,
so long.

Maybe in another lifetime,
maybe we'll meet again;
someday it may be the right time.

1-80

COLD

This cold winter bed
changes color
when you sleep,
lying here beside me.

11-79

ACCEPTANCE

I've already given in to the cold,
bending slightly
into numbness
at the ends of my body,
nose running,
and toes screaming for something warmer.

11-79

MY HUSBAND, I THINK,
IS AN ALCOHOLIC

We look at each other
and try in the mirror
to love one another,
but what of the contact?
Who do we talk to,
if I can't talk to you?
To the cork of this bottle,
while linking mile-long chains
of beer-can pop tops,
patiently waiting
for someone to save me.

5-79

REFLECTIONS ON A
FAILED RELATIONSHIP

My beard isn't as thick
as it's been before.
Our lives aren't as smooth
as we once knew.
The nails on your hands
aren't as long anymore.
The women I see
don't care much for me.
Lines in your face are so strong,
much more than before.
I don't talk so damn slick anymore.

1-79

WOODCUT

Chainsaw slashing,
cutting,
hacking,
pushing,
snaking,
between branches breaking.

Trees scream for mercy,
but it's okay today.
Stretch your branches,
grow new leaves,
so relax, you trees;
I'm only cutting deadwood.

1-79

WINTER UPON US

Winds push trees aside,
circle to rest, carry on.
Leaves soon to fall,
still hold on
to the tree's life blood.
Cold is too soon upon us,
winter's storms,
cold rawness.
Summer's heat now seems so sweet.

10-78

ALONE

At lonesome's pit,
while watching it,
ready to quit,
I sit.

I turn around,
she's looking back,
seems I've found
company.

9-78

ON THE ROAD

I'm traveling around,
windswept window,
round and round,
adjust the mirror,
a washed-out canyon,
up the hill, down.

Each day the window
is a different picture,
each day my vision
adjusts to clearer.

Such powerful pitfalls,
these dreams I hold dear,
yet the drearier life becomes
traveling alone.

Life as it was,
a fleeting glance,
life because
I took the chance,
left the norm,
went on the road.
These circles I travel are a heavy load.

8-78

LOVER

You don't need me;
I'm feeling free,
but I do love to see you
occasionally.

What I need most
is feeling close,
the warmth of a friend for a lover.

7-78

SEX

Our passion to be,
eventually,
today or tomorrow,
matters little to me,
as long as it be
sometime.

7-78

MOMENTS

People take photos
and try to relate
to their friends at a later date.

Poets take the vision of a moment,
attempt to place it within
the framework of words.

Writers remember to recall it later.

As long as the music flows,
musicians live it.

Life is moment after moment.
We strive to capture each,
riding its crest to the next.

7-78

TRAIL TO NEVADA FALLS

People pass,
slow and fast;
some smoke grass,
some with packs,
others with sacks,
always lack
something.

Some will stop,
others walk,
while others talk,
yelling.

Some to see,
some to pee,
oh, please, oh, please,
let me be.

6-78

BROAD STREET

A couple walks arm in arm,
pauses and stares in a store window.
Maybe they see what they might
spend their hard cash on,
in trade for a memory
of what they wished
had been a good time.

5-78

HARDROCK LOWBALL

Set the chips perfectly;
stack them neat,
collect the fee,
the dealer man,
the bank;
I've got the key.
The lowball man,
they pay for me.
I'm important,
don't you see?

12-77

THE WIND

Wind pushes hard against tree limbs,
lightly touches flower stems,
the whistling sound it makes,
which some can barely hear,
in perfect pitch, to me so clear.

10-76

NON-SEX

What frustration I feel.
We make love, eyes to heal,
but don't touch.
I might steal love from you
without the seal
of Good Housekeeping.

9-74

MONEY, TOO

She loves me for my money,
but I have none.

2-74

Channeling Biker Bob has the heart of an anthem. . .
Both men and women can not only enjoy, but perhaps
even take strength from. This novel is the start of
something larger: you can feel it. It's exciting watching
the beginning.

Voted best books in 2001   **January Magazine**

"An intriguing blend of mysticism and adventure. . ."
     Thunder Press

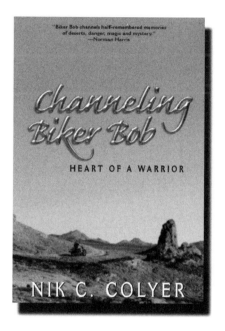

Channeling Biker Bob *Heart of a Warrior*

Nik C. Colyer's
first novel
in the four part series.
Available through your local bookstore for $13.95
or
www.ChannelingBikerBob.com
($13.95 including tax and shipping)

"A superb men and women relationship book in disguise. . . life in its most realistic, rawest form with no holds barred. . .a tough, no nonsense combination of *Men are from Mars and Women are from Venus* and *Iron John.*" **Heartland Review**

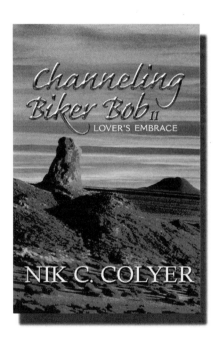